Bird Community Monitoring at Tallgrass Prairie National Preserve, Kansas

2001-2010 Status Report

Natural Resource Data Series NPS/HTLN/NRDS—2011/165

David G. Peitz

National Park Service
The Heartland I&M Network
Wilson's Creek National Battlefield
6424 West Farm Road 182,
Republic, MO 65738

May 2011

U.S. Department of the Interior
National Park Service
Natural Resource Program Center
Fort Collins, Colorado

The National Park Service, Natural Resource Program Center publishes a range of reports that address natural resource topics of interest and applicability to a broad audience in the National Park Service and others in natural resource management, including scientists, conservation and environmental constituencies, and the public.

The Natural Resource Data Series is intended for the timely release of basic data sets and data summaries. Care has been taken to assure accuracy of raw data values, but a thorough analysis and interpretation of the data has not been completed. Consequently, the initial analyses of data in this report are provisional and subject to change.

All manuscripts in the series receive the appropriate level of peer review to ensure that the information is scientifically credible, technically accurate, appropriately written for the intended audience, and designed and published in a professional manner. Data in this report were collected and analyzed using methods based on established, peer-reviewed protocols and were analyzed and interpreted within the guidelines of the protocols.

Views, statements, findings, conclusions, recommendations, and data in this report do not necessarily reflect views and policies of the National Park Service, U.S. Department of the Interior. Mention of trade names or commercial products does not constitute endorsement or recommendation for use by the U.S. Government.

This report is available from Heartland Network I&M Program website (http://www.nature.nps.gov/im/units/HTLN) and the Natural Resource Publications Management website (http://www.nature.nps.gov/publications/NRPM).

Please cite this publication as:

NPS 031/107708, May 2011

Contents

Figures

Tables

Introduction

Birds are an important component of park ecosystems, as their high body temperature, rapid metabolism, and high ecological position in most food webs make them good indicators of the effects of local and regional changes in ecosystems. It has been suggested that management activities aimed at preserving habitat for bird populations, such as for neotropical migrants, can have the added benefit of preserving entire ecosystems and their attendant ecosystem services (Karr 1991, Maurer 1993). Moreover, birds have a tremendous following among the public and many parks provide information on the status and trends of birds through their interpretive programs.

We use trends in the composition and abundance of bird populations as long-term indicators of ecosystem integrity in the habitat of Tallgrass Prairie National Preserve, Kansas (TAPR). Ecosystem integrity is defined as the system's capability to support and maintain a balanced, integrated, adaptive community of organisms having a species composition, diversity, and functional organization comparable to that of the natural habitat of the region (Karr and Dudley 1981). Research has demonstrated that birds serve as good indicators of changes in ecosystems (Cairns et al. 2004, Mallory et al. 2006, Wood et al. 2006).

Therefore, changes in the population size and community composition of birds on the Preserve may reflect the effectiveness of management in restoring and maintaining the grassland and riparian communities at TAPR. Long-term trends in community composition and abundance of breeding bird populations provide one measure for assessing the ecological integrity and sustainability of these systems.

Methods

Site Selection for Bird Plots

Permanent monitoring locations or 'plots' were created by overlaying a systematic grid of 400 x 400 meter cells (originating from a random start point) across the grassland habitat on the Preserve. The orientation of the systematic grid was rotated 34 degrees from north to prevent sampling sites from being influenced by man-made features oriented along cardinal directions. Riparian corridors were identified as a separate stratum, with sampling extending 125 m on either side of the stream channel (Palmer and Fox Creeks). The riparian stratum makes up 5.3% of the total area (4398 ha) at TAPR. Within the riparian stratum, plots were located at 250 m intervals along the extent of a stream. Any plots from the overall park grid that fell within the riparian stratum were discarded. We established 242 grassland (including brome plots) and 18 riparian plots (Figure 1).

During bird surveys, monitoring plots were located using navigation waypoints (Peitz et al. 2010) in a GPS unit and temporarily marked with 36-inch pin flags to aid in re-locating the plots for habitat assessment, eliminating the need for permanent plot markers. We collected pin flags from each plot once the habitat work was completed. Monitoring plots were re-located each year a bird survey was conducted.

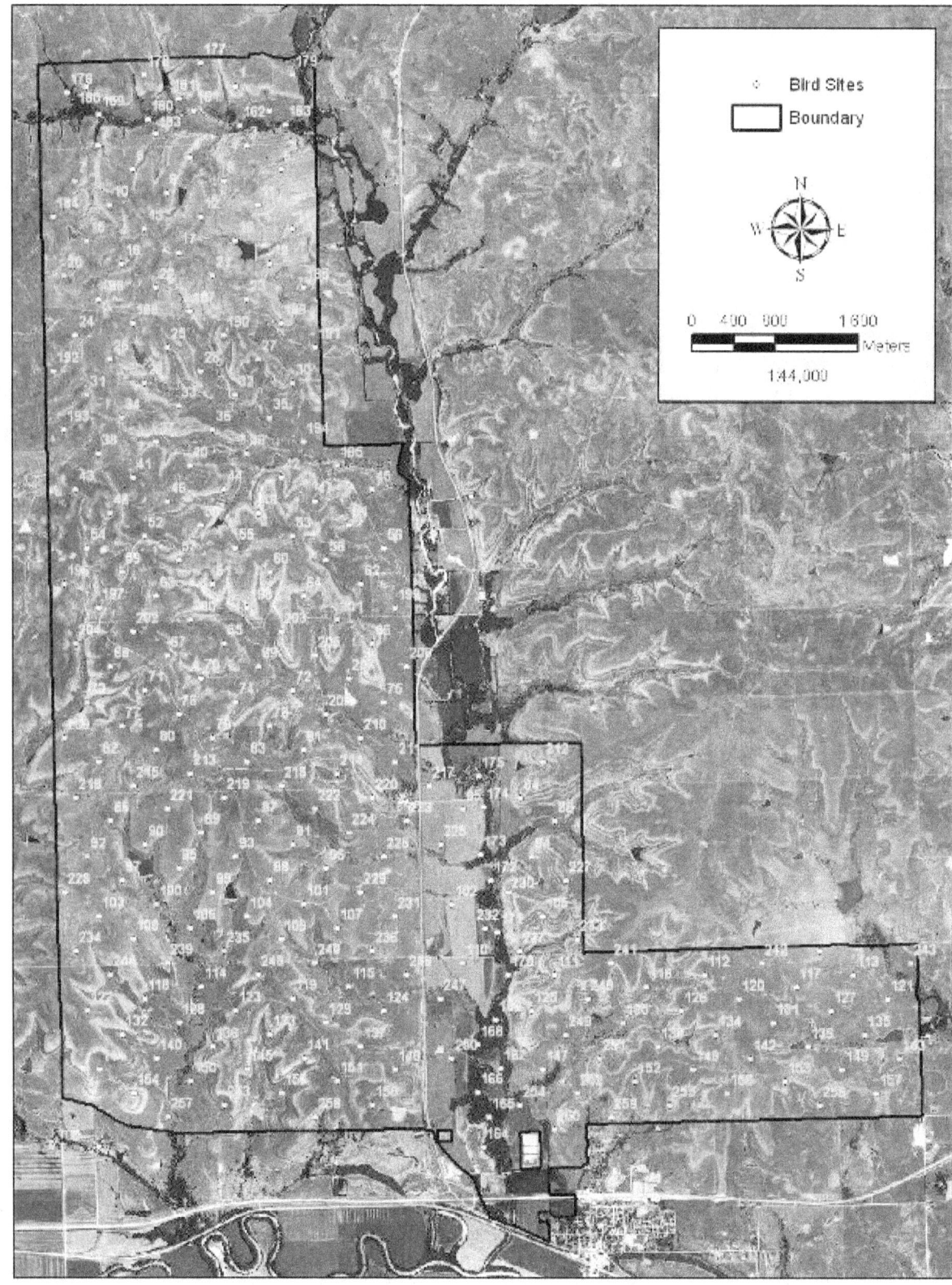

Figure 1. Bird plot locations on Tallgrass Prairie National Preserve, Kansas.

Bird Surveys

Bird surveys followed methods outlined in the bird monitoring protocol by Peitz et al. (2008) and summarized below. Variable circular plot counts, a point count methodology that incorporates a measure of detectability into population estimates, were used to survey birds present (Fancy 1997). All birds seen or heard at plots during 5-min sampling periods were counted along with their corresponding distance from observer. Bird observations were separated into two time segments: those detected during the first three minutes of the count (to allow future comparisons with the national Breeding Bird Survey data), and any new birds detected during the final two minutes of the count. For most species, we recorded each individual bird as a separate observation. For species that usually occur in clusters or flocks, the units recorded were cluster or flock size, and not the individual bird. During analysis, each individual in a cluster or flock was treated as a separate observations. After completing a count at a plot, and filling out the data sheet, the observer(s) navigated to the next plot using a GPS unit. While traveling between plots, the observer(s) was vigilant for the presence of species not recorded during timed surveys. These species help formulate a more complete species list for the park by identifying species missed during timed surveys. We sampled birds during a period when it was light enough to observe birds to four hours after sunrise. Bird surveys were conducted by Heartland Network I&M Program staff in all years except 2009, park staff completed surveys that year.

Bird Habitat

The collection of habitat data followed methods outlined in the bird monitoring protocol by Peitz et al. (2008). A summary of the sampling methods follows. Habitat data collection started after the first variable circular plot count was completed. Observers visited plots for habitat measures in the same order they were surveyed for birds to avoid disturbing birds on a plot prior to the survey. Once the habitat crew arrived at a plot, they set up the center subplot and completed all habitat measures for this subplot and the 50-m radius plot.

We characterized habitat available for each bird species on a number of different scales. Slope, slope variability, aspect, aspect variability, and topographic position of each 50-m radius plot were determined and recorded first. Measurements were recorded during this first year of monitoring, and will not be re-measured in subsequent years (Peitz et al. 2010). The amount of various vegetation types (brome field, corn field, drainage, field/prairie, old field, upland prairie, pond, restored prairie, riparian prairie, riparian woodland, seep, or shrub) and the amount of road and water cover on each plot sampled were recorded. As plots were sampled, horizontal vegetation cover was estimated in 0.50-m (2001-2007, excluding 2003) or 0.25-m (2008, 2010) intervals from 0.0 to 2.0 meters above ground surface using a 0.15-cm wide cover board. Area of the cover board obscured by vegetation was estimated at a 15-m distances from plot center. Using a graduated measuring rod, vertical vegetation structure was measured in 1-m increments up to 7.5 meters in height at four locations around the perimeter of the subplot. Locations were in the four cardinal directions. Vertical structure was recorded for deciduous and herbaceous vegetation. Trees were tallied by species and size class (<1.0 cm, 1.1 – 2.5 cm, 2.6 – 8.0 cm, 8.1 – 15.0 cm, 15.1 – 23.0 cm, 23.1 – 38.0 or >38.0 cm) on the subplot. Lastly, at the subplot, ground and foliar cover were recorded in a 1.78-m radius nested sample plot. Ground cover included deciduous and grass litter, bare soil, rock, woody debris (>2.5 cm diameter), and unvegetated. Foliar cover was estimated for six plant guilds, including warm- and cool-season grasses, forbs, moss and lichens, shrubs and vines, tree seedlings, and total foliar cover (<1.5 m tall). Average parameter values were reported for the Preserve for grassland (including brome habitat) and riparian habitats, annually.

Data Analysis

Prior to summary analysis, the residency status (permanent resident, summer resident, migrant, species out of their normal range, and winter resident) of each bird species recorded was determined. Identifying the residency of each species helps to exclude migrants, species out of their normal range, and winter residents from analysis of breeding birds within TAPR. Hereafter, permanent and summer resident birds are referred to as breeding species. The frequency and abundance of breeding bird species were determined two ways. First, for each breeding species, the number of individuals encountered per plot visit was determined (individuals/plot visit). And second, the proportion of plots occupied by each breeding species was determined (total number of plots occupied by a species/total number of plots visited).

Location and permanent abiotic measures on each plot and habitat subplot were reported (Peitz et al. 2010). Annual averages (± std dev) for semi-permanent plot data, including road and water cover were calculated from plot estimates for both grassland and riparian habitats. In 2001 and 2002, using plot values, averages (± std dev) for horizontal vegetation cover between 0 – 0.50, 0.5 – 1.0, 1.0 – 1.50, and 1.5 – 2.00 meters were calculated by habitat type. Between 2004 and 2007, using plot values, averages (± std dev) for horizontal vegetation cover between 0 – 0.50, 0.25-0.75, 0.5 – 1.0, 0.75-1.25, 1.0 – 1.50, 1.25-1.75, and 1.5 – 2.00 meters were calculated by habitat type. In 2008 and 2010, using plot values, averages (± std dev) for horizontal vegetation cover between 0 – 0.25, 0.25-0.5, 0.5 – 0.75, 0.75-1.0, 1.0 – 1.25, 1.25-1.5, 1.5 – 1.75, and 1.75 – 2.0 meters were calculated by habitat type. Average (±std dev) height of vegetation on plots in the grassland habitat was measured and reported. Average (± std dev) annual vertical structure diversity was estimated and reported by habitat type as well.

$$\text{Structural Diversity Index} = \frac{((\sum p_i / 8) + a) * 100}{2}$$

Where p_i – is the observed frequency for vegetation in the ith interval touching a measuring rod out of twelve measuring events, and a – is the percent of intervals with recorded vegetation in eight height increments. Vertical structure diversity values are weighted equally to represent both the vertical height of vegetation and how dense the vegetation is within each height increment.

Within each plot, ground cover, including deciduous and grass litter, bare soil, rock, woody debris (>2.5 cm DBH), and unvegetated were averaged (± std dev) across plots within each habitat type. Foliar cover, by guild of warm- and cool-season grasses, forbs, mosses and lichens, shrubs and vines, tree seedlings and total foliar cover (<1.5 m tall) were averaged (± std dev) across plots within habitat types as well. Composition and size classes of trees in the riparian habitat are reported to family.

Results

Bird Surveys

Ninety-seven avian species were recorded on TAPR during breeding bird surveys in 2001-2010, excluding 2003 (Table 1). Eighty-two of the 97 species are year round or summer residents (Stokes and Stokes 1996). Four species, Brown Creeper (*Certhia americana*), Eastern Towhee (*Pipilo erythrophthalmus*), Song Sparrow (*Melospiza melodia*), and Yellow-bellied Sapsucker (*Sphyrapicus varius*) are winter residents to the Preserve. Nine species, Bobolink (*Dolichonyx oryzivorus*), Northern Parula (*Parula americana*), Scarlet Tanager (*Piranga olivacea*), Sedge Wren (*Cistothorus platensis*), Semipalmated Sandpiper (*Calidris pusilla*), Summer Tanager (*Piranga rubra*), Veery (*Catharus fuscescens*), Vesper Sparrow (*Pooecetes gramineus*), and Wood Duck (*Aix sponsa*) are migrants through the area. Two additional species recorded on the Preserve, Eurasian Collared-dove (*Streptopelia decaocto*) and Golden-winged Warbler (*Vermivora chrysoptera*) are outside of their normal range. Three breeding species, Great Egret (*Casmerodius albus*), Spotted Sandpiper (*Actitis macularia*), and Warbling Vireo (*Vireo gilvus*) were only recorded outside of 5-min survey periods.

On TAPR, Acadian Flycatcher (*Empidonax virescens*), Brown Thrasher (*Toxostoma rufum*), Carolina Wren (*Thryothorus ludovicianus*), Dickcissel (*Spiza americana*), Grasshopper Sparrow (*Ammodramus savannarum*), Greater Prairie-chicken (*Tympanuchus cupido*), Henslow's Sparrow (*Ammodramus henslowii*), Indigo Bunting (*Passerina cyanea*), Prothonotary Warbler (*Protonotaria citrea*), Red-bellied Woodpecker (*Melanerpes carolinus*), Red-headed Woodpecker (*Melanerpes erythrocephalus*), White-eyed Vireo (*Vireo griseus*), and Yellow-throated Vireo (*Vireo flavifrons*) are breeding species of continental importance (Rich et al. 2004). The Eastern Towhee, Golden-winged Warbler, and Yellow-bellied Sapsucker are species of continental importance as well. Nine breeding species, Dickcissel, Eastern Meadowlark (*Sturnella magna*), Grasshopper Sparrow, Greater Prairie-chicken, Henslow's Sparrow, Horned Lark (*Eremophila alpestris*), Northern Harrier (*Circus cyaneus*), Upland Sandpiper (*Bartramia longicauda*), and Western meadowlark (*Sturnella neglecta*) are grassland obligates. Bobolink, Sedge Wren, and Vesper Sparrow are grassland obligate species as well.

Brown-headed cowbird (*Molothrus ater*), Dickcissel, Grasshopper Sparrow, Eastern and/or Western Meadowlark, Red-winged Blackbird (*Agelaius phoeniceus*), and Upland Sandpiper are the most commonly encountered and widely distributed species in the grassland habitat on the Preserve, annually (Table 2 and 3). Great Crested Flycatcher (*Myiarchus crinitus*), Eastern Wood-pewee (*Contopus virens*), Northern Cardinal (*Cardinalis cardinalis*), and Red-bellied Woodpecker are the most commonly encountered and widely distributed species in the riparian habitat on the Preserve, annually (Table 2 and 3).

Table 1. Species recorded at Tallgrass Prairie National Preserve, Kansas during breeding bird surveys, years 2001-2010, excluding 2003.

Common name	Species name	AOU code	Residency Status[1]
Acadian Flycatcher	*Empidonax virescens*	**ACFL**	**SR**
American Crow	*Corvus brachyrhynchos*	AMCR	R
American Goldfinch	*Carduelis tristis*	AMGO	R
American Robin	*Turdus migratorius*	AMRO	R
Bank Swallow	*Riparia riparia*	BANS	SR
Barn Swallow	*Hirundo rustica*	BARS	SR
Barred Owl	*Strix varia*	BDOW	R
Belted Kingfisher	*Megaceryle alcyon*	BEKI	R
Bewick's Wren	*Thryomanes bewickii*	BEWR	R
Black-billed Cuckoo	*Coccyzus erythropthalmus*	BBCU	SR
Black-capped Chickadee	*Poecile atricapillus*	BCCH	R
Blue-gray Gnatcatcher	*Polioptila caerulea*	BGGN	SR
Blue Grosbeak	*Guiraca caerulea*	BLGR	SR
Blue Jay	*Cyanocitta cristata*	BLJA	R
Bobolink*	*Dolichonyx oryzivorus*	BOBO	M
Brown Creeper	*Certhia americana*	BRCR	WR
Brown-headed Cowbird	*Molothrus ater*	BHCO	R
Brown Thrasher	*Toxostoma rufum*	**BRTH**	**R**
Canada Goose	*Branta canadensis*	CAGO	R
Carolina Chickadee	*Parus carolinensis*	CACH	R
Carolina Wren	*Thryothorus ludovicianus*	**CARW**	**R**
Cattle Egret	*Bubulcus ibis*	CAEG	SR
Cliff Swallow	*Petrochelidon pyrrhonota*	CLSW	SR
Common Grackle	*Quiscalus quiscula*	COGR	R
Common Nighthawk	*Chordeiles minor*	CONI	SR
Common Yellowthroat	*Geothlypis trichas*	COYE	SR
Dickcissel*	*Spiza americana*	**DICK**	**SR**
Downy Woodpecker	*Picoides pubescens*	DOWO	R
Eastern Bluebird	*Sialia sialis*	EABL	R
Eastern Kingbird	*Tyrannus tyrannus*	EAKI	SR
Eastern Meadowlark*	*Sturnella magna*	EAME	R
Eastern Phoebe	*Sayornis phoebe*	EAPH	SR
Eastern (Rufous-side) Towhee	*Pipilo erythrophthalmus*	**EATO**	**WR**
Eastern Wood-pewee	*Contopus virens*	EAWP	SR
Eurasian Collared-dove**	*Streptopelia decaocto*	ECDO	O
Field Sparrow	*Spizella pusilla*	FISP	R
Golden-winged Warbler	*Vermivora chrysoptera*	**GWWA**	**O**
Grasshopper Sparrow*	*Ammodramus savannarum*	**GRSP**	**SR**
Gray Catbird	*Dumetella carolinensis*	GRCA	SR
Great Blue Heron	*Ardea herodias*	GBHE	R
Great Crested Flycatcher	*Myiarchus crinitus*	GCFL	SR
Great Horned Owl	*Bubo virginianus*	GHOW	R

Table 1. Species recorded at Tallgrass Prairie National Preserve, Kansas during breeding bird surveys, years 2001-2010, excluding 2003 (continued).

Common name	Species name	AOU code	Residency Status[1]
Great Egret**	*Casmerodius albus*	GREG	SR
Great-tailed Grackle	*Quiscalus mexicanus*	GTGR	SR
Greater Prairie-chicken*	***Tympanuchus cupido***	**GPCH**	**R**
Hairy Woodpecker	*Picoides villosus*	HAWO	R
Henslow's Sparrow*	***Ammodramus henslowii***	**HESP**	**SR**
Horned Lark*	*Eremophila alpestris*	HOLA	R
House Wren	*Troglodytes aedon*	HOWR	SR
Indigo Bunting	***Passerina cyanea***	**INBU**	**SR**
Killdeer	*Charadrius vociferous*	KILL	R
Lark Sparrow	*Chondestes grammacus*	LASP	SR
Loggerhead Shrike	*Lanius ludovicianus*	LOSH	R
Mallard	*Anas platyrhynchos*	MALL	R
Mourning Dove	*Zenaida macroura*	MODO	R
Northern Bobwhite	*Colinus virginianus*	NOBO	R
Northern Cardinal	*Cardinalis cardinalis*	NOCA	R
Northern (Yellow-shafted) Flicker	*Colaptes auratus*	YSFL	R
Northern Harrier*	*Circus cyaneus*	NOHA	R
Northern Mockingbird	*Minus polyglottos*	NOMO	R
Northern (Baltimore) Oriole	*Icterus galbula*	BAOR	SR
Northern Parula	*Parula americana*	NOPA	M
Northern Rough-winged Swallow	*Stelgidopteryx serripennis*	NRWS	SR
Orchard Oriole	*Icterus spurius*	OROR	SR
Pied-billed Grebe	*Podilymbus podiceps*	PBGR	SR
Prothonotary Warbler	***Protonotaria citrea***	**PROW**	**SR**
Red-bellied Woodpecker	***Melanerpes carolinus***	**RBWO**	**R**
Red-eyed Vireo	*Vireo olivaceus*	REVI	SR
Red-headed Woodpecker	***Melanerpes erythrocephalus***	**RHWO**	**R**
Red-tailed Hawk	*Buteo jamaicensis*	RTHA	R
Red-winged Blackbird	*Agelaius phoeniceus*	RWBL	R
Ring-necked Pheasant	*Phasianus colchicus*	RPHE	R
Ruby-throated Hummingbird	*Archilochus colubris*	RTHU	SR
Scarlet Tanager	*Piranga olivacea*	SCTA	M
Scissor-tailed Flycatcher	*Tyrannus forficatus*	STFL	SR
Sedge Wren*	*Cistothorus platensis*	SEWR	M
Semipalmated Sandpiper**	*Calidris pusilla*	SESA	M
Spotted Sandpiper**	*Actitis macularia*	SPSA	SR
Song Sparrow**	*Melospiza melodia*	SOSP	WR
Summer Tanager	*Piranga rubra*	SUTA	M
(Eastern) Tufted Titmouse	*Baeolophus bicolor*	ETTI	R
Turkey Vulture	*Cathartes aura*	TUVU	SR
Upland Sandpiper*	*Bartramia longicauda*	UPSA	SR
Veery	*Catharus fuscescens*	VEER	M

Table 1. Species recorded at Tallgrass Prairie National Preserve, Kansas during breeding bird surveys, years 2001-2010, excluding 2003 (continued).

Common name	Species name	AOU code	Residency Status[1]
Vesper Sparrow*	*Pooecetes gramineus*	VESP	M
Warbling Vireo**	*Vireo gilvus*	WAVI	SR
Western Kingbird	*Tyrannus verticalis*	WEKI	SR
Western Meadowlark*	*Sturnella neglecta*	WEME	R
White-breasted Nuthatch	*Sitta carolinensis*	WBNU	R
White-eyed Vireo	***Vireo griseus***	**WEVI**	**SR**
Wild Turkey	*Meleagris gallopavo*	WITU	R
Wood Duck	*Aix sponsa*	WODU	M
Yellow-bellied Sapsucker	***Sphyrapicus varius***	**YBSA**	**WR**
Yellow-billed Cuckoo	*Coccyzus americanus*	YBCU	SR
Yellow-breasted Chat	*Icteria virens*	YBCH	SR
Yellow-throated Vireo	***Vireo flavifrons***	**YTVI**	**SR**
Yellow Warbler	*Dendroica petechia*	YWAR	SR

* Obligate grassland species. These species require relatively treeless grasslands for all or most of their breeding cycle (Northern Prairie Wildlife Research Center. Accessed in 2009, http://www.npwrc.usgs.gov/).

** Species recorded only while traveling between point transects or at other times outside of 5-min survey periods.

[1] Residency status: SR = summer resident; R = year around resident; M = late season migrant; WR = winter resident; O = outside of normal range. According to Stokes and Stokes (1996).

Species names are valid and verified names obtained from ITIS in 2010 (Integrated Taxonomic Information System http://www.itis.gov/).

Bolded species names are those species considered of continental importance (Rich et al. 2004).

Table 2. Number of individuals encountered per plot visit, over all plots sampled each year, for breeding bird species recorded at Tallgrass Prairie National Preserve, Kansas during the 2001-2010 (excluding 2003) breeding bird surveys, by habitat type. Number of individuals per plot includes all individuals recorded on plots during a 5-min survey, including flyovers.

Common name	Individual/plot visit								
	Grassland								
	2001	2002	2004	2005	2006	2007	2008	2009	2010
	n=158	n=242	n=81	n=79	n=81	n=71	n=77	n=40	n=242
Acadian Flycatcher	0.00	0.01	0.00	0.00	0.00	0.00	0.00	0.00	0.00
American Crow	0.00	0.08	0.07	0.06	0.10	0.04	0.00	0.05	>0.01
American Goldfinch	0.00	0.01	0.00	0.00	0.00	0.00	0.00	0.00	>0.01
American Robin	0.00	0.00	0.00	0.00	0.00	0.00	0.00	0.00	0.01
Bank Swallow	<0.01	0.06	0.09	0.08	0.02	0.00	0.09	0.00	0.14
Barn Swallow	0.05	0.03	0.25	0.11	0.23	0.01	0.01	0.35	0.15
Bewick's Wren	0.00	0.01	0.01	0.01	0.00	0.01	0.01	0.00	0.00
Black-billed Cuckoo	0.00	0.00	0.00	0.01	0.00	0.00	0.00	0.00	0.00
Black-capped Chickadee	0.00	0.01	0.01	0.00	0.00	0.00	0.00	0.00	0.00
Blue-gray Gnatcatcher	<0.01	0.00	0.00	0.00	0.00	0.00	0.00	0.00	0.00
Blue Jay	0.03	0.06	0.02	0.05	0.09	0.07	0.00	0.05	>0.01
Brown-headed Cowbird	0.65	1.14	0.90	0.97	0.89	0.83	0.74	0.80	0.96
Brown Thrasher	0.02	0.06	0.10	0.03	0.07	0.03	0.03	0.03	0.04
Canada Goose	0.00	0.07	0.21	0.01	0.10	0.03	0.03	0.00	0.01
Carolina Wren	0.00	0.00	0.00	0.00	0.00	0.00	0.01	0.00	0.00
Cattle Egret	0.03	0.00	0.00	0.00	0.00	0.00	0.00	0.00	0.00
Cliff Swallow	0.14	0.01	0.00	0.00	0.00	0.01	0.00	0.10	0.07
Common Grackle	0.01	<0.01	0.01	0.01	0.02	0.00	0.00	0.00	0.00
Common Nighthawk	0.16	0.25	0.05	0.47	0.15	0.23	0.09	0.10	0.10
Common Yellowthroat	0.00	<0.01	0.00	0.00	0.00	0.00	0.00	0.00	0.01
Dickcissel	0.71	0.82	0.69	0.86	1.48	1.01	1.61	1.88	0.99
Downy Woodpecker	0.00	0.01	0.00	0.00	0.00	0.00	0.00	0.00	0.00
Eastern Bluebird	0.01	0.00	0.00	0.04	0.00	0.01	0.05	0.03	>0.01
Eastern Kingbird	0.02	0.05	0.07	0.09	0.15	0.14	0.01	0.10	0.02
Eastern Meadowlark	0.26	0.02	0.01	0.00	0.00	0.03	0.64	1.33	1.29
Eastern Phoebe	0.00	<0.01	0.02	0.00	0.00	0.00	0.00	0.00	0.00
Eastern Wood-pewee	0.00	0.01	0.00	0.01	0.00	0.00	0.01	0.00	0.01
Field Sparrow	0.00	<0.01	0.00	0.00	0.00	0.00	0.00	0.00	0.01
Grasshopper Sparrow	1.04	0.86	1.05	1.03	0.95	1.15	1.23	0.95	0.89
Great Blue Heron	0.01	0.01	0.04	0.04	0.04	0.03	0.03	0.08	0.02
Great Crested Flycatcher	0.00	0.03	0.15	0.06	0.04	0.07	0.04	0.00	0.03
Great Horned Owl	0.00	<0.01	0.00	0.00	0.00	0.00	0.00	0.00	>0.01
Great-tailed Grackle	0.01	0.00	0.02	0.01	0.00	0.00	0.00	0.03	0.00
Greater Prairie-chicken	0.03	0.04	0.01	0.00	0.01	0.00	0.01	0.00	0.18
Hairy Woodpecker	0.01	0.00	0.00	0.00	0.00	0.00	0.00	0.00	0.00
Henslow's Sparrow	0.00	0.00	0.00	0.00	0.02	0.01	0.18	0.15	0.12
Horned Lark	0.02	0.00	0.38	0.11	0.12	0.06	0.00	0.03	0.04

Table 2. Number of individuals encountered per plot visit, over all plots sampled each year, for breeding bird species recorded at Tallgrass Prairie National Preserve, Kansas during the 2001-2010 (excluding 2003) breeding bird surveys, by habitat type. Number of individuals per plot includes all individuals recorded on plots during a 5-min survey, including flyovers (continued).

Common name	Individuals/plot visit								
	Grassland								
	2001	2002	2004	2005	2006	2007	2008	2009	2010
	n=158	n=242	n=81	n=79	n=81	n=71	n=77	n=40	n=242
Indigo Bunting	0.00	<0.01	0.00	0.00	0.00	0.00	0.00	0.00	0.00
Killdeer	0.08	0.13	0.20	0.33	0.25	0.17	0.10	0.05	0.09
Lark Sparrow	0.02	0.10	0.11	0.09	0.02	0.14	0.09	0.00	0.03
Loggerhead Shrike	0.00	<0.01	0.00	0.00	0.00	0.00	0.00	0.00	0.00
Mallard	0.00	0.00	0.00	0.00	0.00	0.00	0.00	0.00	>0.01
Mourning Dove	0.10	0.07	0.01	0.01	0.02	0.08	0.10	0.10	0.06
Northern Bobwhite	0.00	0.04	0.05	0.10	0.20	0.08	0.08	0.28	0.05
Northern Cardinal	0.00	0.05	0.01	0.03	0.01	0.03	0.00	0.00	>0.01
Northern Flicker	0.00	<0.01	0.01	0.00	0.00	0.00	0.00	0.03	0.00
Northern Harrier	0.00	0.00	0.00	0.01	0.00	0.01	0.00	0.00	0.01
Northern Mockingbird	0.00	0.00	0.00	0.03	0.01	0.01	0.00	0.05	0.03
Northern Oriole	0.00	0.00	0.00	0.04	0.02	0.08	0.06	0.03	0.02
Northern Rough-winged Swallow	0.01	0.00	0.00	0.00	0.00	0.00	0.00	0.00	>0.01
Orchard Oriole	0.01	0.01	0.00	0.00	0.07	0.00	0.03	0.00	0.04
Pied-billed Grebe	0.00	0.00	0.00	0.00	0.01	0.00	0.00	0.00	0.00
Red-bellied Woodpecker	0.01	0.4	0.02	0.03	0.00	0.01	0.00	0.00	0.00
Red-headed Woodpecker	0.00	0.00	0.00	0.00	0.04	0.00	0.00	0.03	>0.01
Red-tailed Hawk	0.00	0.00	0.01	0.01	0.00	0.01	0.00	0.00	0.00
Red-winged Blackbird	0.17	0.35	0.48	0.41	0.33	0.48	0.14	0.43	0.19
Ring-neck Pheasant	0.00	0.00	0.00	0.00	0.00	0.00	0.00	0.03	0.00
Scissor-tailed Flycatcher	0.00	0.01	0.05	0.03	0.06	0.07	0.00	0.00	0.00
Tufted Titmouse	0.00	0.07	0.02	0.00	0.02	0.03	0.01	0.00	0.01
Turkey Vulture	0.01	0.02	0.01	0.03	0.05	0.01	0.03	0.20	0.17
Upland Sandpiper	0.41	1.10	1.10	0.76	0.73	0.54	0.56	0.55	0.27
Western Kingbird	0.02	0.00	0.00	0.00	0.00	0.00	0.00	0.00	>0.01
Western Meadowlark	0.26	1.06	1.58	1.97	1.60	1.18	0.78	0.00	0.04
White-breasted Nuthatch	0.00	0.02	0.00	0.01	0.00	0.00	0.00	0.00	0.00
White-eyed Vireo	0.00	0.00	0.00	0.00	0.00	0.00	0.00	0.00	0.01
Wild Turkey	0.00	<0.01	0.01	0.00	0.00	0.00	0.00	0.00	0.03
Yellow-billed Cuckoo	0.00	0.04	0.02	0.00	0.00	0.00	0.00	0.00	0.00
Yellow-breasted Chat	0.00	0.03	0.00	0.00	0.00	0.00	0.00	0.00	0.00
Yellow-throated Vireo	0.00	0.01	0.01	0.00	0.00	0.00	0.00	0.00	0.00
Yellow Warbler	0.13	0.00	0.00	0.00	0.00	0.00	0.00	0.00	0.00

Table 2. Number of individuals encountered per plot visit, over all plots sampled each year, for breeding bird species recorded at Tallgrass Prairie National Preserve, Kansas during the 2001-2010 (excluding 2003) breeding bird surveys, by habitat type. Number of individuals per plot includes all individuals recorded on plots during a 5-min survey, including flyovers (continued).

Common name	Individuals/plot visit								
	Riparian								
	2001	2002	2004	2005	2006	2007	2008	2009	2010
	n=18	n=18	n=16	n=18	n=18	n=18	n=18	n=18	n=18
Acadian Flycatcher	**0.00**	**0.28**	**0.00**	**0.00**	**0.00**	**0.00**	**0.00**	**0.00**	**0.00**
American Crow	0.06	0.28	0.00	0.06	0.06	0.06	0.06	0.06	0.00
American Goldfinch	0.22	0.00	0.00	0.00	0.00	0.00	0.00	0.00	0.28
American Robin	0.00	0.00	0.06	0.00	0.00	0.00	0.00	0.17	0.11
Bank Swallow	0.00	0.00	0.25	0.00	0.00	0.00	0.17	0.00	0.11
Barn Swallow	0.00	0.00	0.00	0.06	0.00	0.00	0.00	0.00	0.00
Barred Owl	0.11	0.00	0.00	0.39	0.00	0.00	0.00	0.00	0.00
Belted Kingfisher	0.06	0.00	0.06	0.06	0.00	0.06	0.06	0.00	0.06
Bewick's Wren	0.11	0.11	0.06	0.06	0.00	0.11	0.17	0.00	0.00
Black-billed Cuckoo	0.06	0.06	0.00	0.44	0.00	0.00	0.00	0.00	0.00
Black-capped Chickadee	0.11	0.67	0.25	0.11	0.00	0.00	0.00	0.06	0.00
Blue-gray Gnatcatcher	0.06	0.00	0.13	0.28	0.28	0.17	0.28	0.11	0.11
Blue Grosbeak	0.00	0.00	0.19	0.00	0.00	0.00	0.06	0.00	0.00
Blue Jay	0.17	0.17	0.19	0.33	0.17	0.17	0.11	0.39	0.06
Brown-headed Cowbird	0.06	0.00	0.00	0.00	0.00	0.06	0.06	0.11	0.00
Brown Thrasher	**0.06**	**0.00**	**0.00**	**0.00**	**0.00**	**0.00**	**0.00**	**0.06**	**0.00**
Canada Goose	0.00	0.00	0.00	0.00	0.00	0.11	0.00	0.00	0.00
Carolina Chickadee	0.00	0.00	0.00	0.00	0.00	0.00	0.17	0.00	0.06
Carolina Wren	**0.17**	**0.00**	**0.00**	**0.11**	**0.11**	**0.11**	**0.06**	**0.00**	**0.06**
Cliff Swallow	0.00	0.11	0.00	0.00	0.00	0.00	0.00	0.00	0.00
Common Nighthawk	0.00	0.06	0.00	0.00	0.00	0.00	0.00	0.00	0.00
Common Yellowthroat	0.00	0.28	0.00	0.00	0.00	0.00	0.06	0.00	0.06
Dickcissel	**0.00**	**0.28**	**0.00**	**0.17**	**0.11**	**0.17**	**0.06**	**0.50**	**0.28**
Downy Woodpecker	0.11	0.22	0.00	0.00	0.00	0.00	0.06	0.00	0.06
Eastern Bluebird	0.00	0.00	0.00	0.06	0.22	0.11	0.00	0.11	0.00
Eastern Kingbird	0.00	0.00	0.00	0.00	0.00	0.00	0.06	0.00	0.00
Eastern Meadowlark	0.00	0.00	0.00	0.00	0.00	0.00	0.00	0.11	0.06
Eastern Phoebe	0.00	0.11	0.19	0.06	0.06	0.06	0.06	0.11	0.00
Eastern Wood-pewee	0.33	0.72	0.50	0.78	0.83	0.83	0.33	0.89	0.61
Gray Catbird	0.06	0.00	0.00	0.06	0.00	0.00	0.00	0.00	0.00
Great Blue Heron	0.00	0.00	0.00	0.00	0.00	0.06	0.00	0.17	0.06
Great Crested Flycatcher	0.33	0.33	0.88	0.56	0.72	0.56	0.17	0.22	0.28
Great Horned Owl	0.00	0.00	0.00	0.06	0.00	0.00	0.00	0.00	0.00
Hairy Woodpecker	0.00	0.00	0.19	0.06	0.00	0.00	0.00	0.06	0.00
House Wren	0.00	0.00	0.00	0.00	0.06	0.00	0.00	0.00	0.00
Indigo Bunting	**0.06**	**0.17**	**0.00**	**0.00**	**0.00**	**0.11**	**0.33**	**0.17**	**0.06**
Lark Sparrow	0.00	0.00	0.00	0.00	0.00	0.00	0.06	0.00	0.00

Table 2. Number of individuals encountered per plot visit, over all plots sampled each year, for breeding bird species recorded at Tallgrass Prairie National Preserve, Kansas during the 2001-2010 (excluding 2003) breeding bird surveys, by habitat type. Number of individuals per plot includes all individuals recorded on plots during a 5-min survey, including flyovers (continued).

Common name	Individuals/plot visit								
	Riparian								
	2001	2002	2004	2005	2006	2007	2008	2009	2010
	n=18	n=18	n=16	n=18	n=18	n=18	n=18	n=18	n=18
Mourning Dove	0.00	0.00	0.00	0.06	0.00	0.06	0.22	0.28	0.00
Northern Bobwhite	0.00	0.00	0.00	0.00	0.00	0.00	0.00	0.06	0.00
Northern Cardinal	0.17	0.44	0.25	0.28	0.22	0.33	0.28	0.50	0.22
Northern Flicker	0.00	0.00	0.00	0.06	0.00	0.00	0.00	0.39	0.00
Northern Mockingbird	0.00	0.00	0.00	0.00	0.00	0.00	0.06	0.00	0.00
Northern Oriole	0.00	0.00	0.00	0.39	0.39	0.00	0.06	0.22	0.00
Northern Rough-winged Swallow	0.00	0.00	0.00	0.00	0.00	0.00	0.00	0.00	0.06
Orchard Oriole	0.06	0.11	0.06	0.00	0.06	0.00	0.00	0.00	0.06
Prothonotary Warbler	**0.11**	**0.00**	**0.00**	**0.00**	**0.00**	**0.00**	**0.00**	**0.00**	**0.06**
Red-bellied Woodpecker	**0.17**	**0.39**	**0.25**	**0.22**	**0.39**	**0.17**	**0.28**	**0.17**	**0.17**
Red-eyed Vireo	0.00	0.28	0.19	0.17	0.33	0.22	0.11	0.06	0.17
Red-headed Woodpecker	**0.00**	**0.06**	**0.19**	**0.00**	**0.00**	**0.00**	**0.00**	**0.11**	**0.00**
Red-tailed Hawk	0.00	0.00	0.06	0.00	0.06	0.00	0.00	0.00	0.00
Red-winged Blackbird	0.00	0.17	0.06	0.00	0.00	0.06	0.00	0.00	0.00
Ruby-throated Hummingbird	0.00	0.00	0.00	0.06	0.00	0.00	0.00	0.00	0.00
Tufted Titmouse	0.11	0.56	0.50	0.17	0.39	0.39	0.11	0.00	0.39
Turkey Vulture	0.00	0.00	0.06	0.00	0.00	0.00	0.00	0.06	0.11
Western Meadowlark	0.00	0.11	0.31	0.00	0.11	0.00	0.00	0.00	0.00
White-breasted Nuthatch	0.00	0.44	0.13	0.17	0.28	0.22	0.11	0.17	0.11
White-eyed Vireo	**0.17**	**0.00**	**0.00**	**0.00**	**0.00**	**0.00**	**0.00**	**0.00**	**0.00**
Wild Turkey	0.00	0.00	0.06	0.06	0.00	0.11	0.00	0.06	0.00
Yellow-billed Cuckoo	0.11	0.33	0.81	0.00	0.00	0.06	0.22	0.17	0.00
Yellow-breasted Chat	0.00	0.00	0.00	0.00	0.00	0.06	0.00	0.00	0.00
Yellow-throated Vireo	**0.06**	**0.06**	**0.13**	**0.17**	**0.00**	**0.06**	**0.17**	**0.11**	**0.11**
Yellow Warbler	0.22	0.00	0.25	0.11	0.33	0.0	0.06	0.00	0.06

Bolded species names are those species considered of continental importance (Rich et al. 2004).

Table 3. Proportion of plots occupied annually by breeding bird species (including flyovers) at Tallgrass Prairie National Preserve, Kansas during the 2001-2010 (excluding 2003) breeding bird surveys, by habitat type.

Common name	Proportion of plots occupied								
	Grassland								
	2001	2002	2004	2005	2006	2007	2008	2009	2010
	n=158	n=242	n=81	n=79	n=81	n=71	n=77	n=40	n=242
Acadian Flycatcher	**0.00**	**0.01**	**0.00**	**0.00**	**0.00**	**0.00**	**0.00**	**0.00**	**0.00**
American Crow	0.00	0.06	0.06	0.01	0.05	0.04	0.00	0.05	>0.01
American Goldfinch	0.00	0.01	0.00	0.00	0.00	0.00	0.00	0.00	>0.01
American Robin	0.00	0.00	0.00	0.00	0.00	0.00	0.00	0.00	0.01
Bank Swallow	0.01	0.05	0.05	0.04	0.02	0.00	0.05	0.00	0.06
Barn Swallow	0.04	0.02	0.10	0.10	0.12	0.01	0.01	0.18	0.07
Bewick's Wren	0.00	0.01	0.01	0.01	0.00	0.01	0.01	0.00	0.00
Black-billed Cuckoo	0.00	0.00	0.00	0.01	0.00	0.00	0.00	0.00	0.00
Black-capped Chickadee	0.00	0.01	0.01	0.00	0.00	0.00	0.00	0.00	0.00
Blue-gray Gnatcatcher	0.01	0.00	0.00	0.00	0.00	0.00	0.00	0.00	0.00
Blue Jay	0.01	0.04	0.02	0.05	0.06	0.06	0.00	0.05	>0.01
Brown-headed Cowbird	0.37	0.64	0.42	0.49	0.44	0.51	0.42	0.50	0.47
Brown Thrasher	**0.02**	**0.06**	**0.09**	**0.03**	**0.06**	**0.03**	**0.01**	**0.03**	**0.04**
Canada Goose	0.00	0.01	0.06	0.01	0.06	0.01	0.01	0.00	0.01
Carolina Wren	**0.00**	**0.00**	**0.00**	**0.00**	**0.00**	**0.00**	**0.01**	**0.00**	**0.00**
Cattle Egret	0.01	0.00	0.00	0.00	0.00	0.00	0.00	0.00	0.00
Cliff Swallow	0.08	<0.01	0.00	0.00	0.00	0.01	0.00	0.03	0.02
Common Grackle	0.01	<0.01	0.01	0.01	0.01	0.00	0.00	0.00	0.00
Common Nighthawk	0.11	0.20	0.04	0.32	0.14	0.17	0.09	0.10	0.09
Common Yellowthroat	0.00	<0.01	0.00	0.00	0.00	0.00	0.00	0.00	0.01
Dickcissel	**0.38**	**0.61**	**0.35**	**0.46**	**0.58**	**0.54**	**0.83**	**0.93**	**0.56**
Downy Woodpecker	0.00	0.01	0.00	0.00	0.00	0.00	0.00	0.00	0.00
Eastern Bluebird	0.01	0.00	0.00	0.03	0.00	0.01	0.01	0.03	>0.01
Eastern Kingbird	0.02	0.05	0.06	0.05	0.09	0.10	0.01	0.08	0.01
Eastern Meadowlark	0.18	0.02	0.01	0.00	0.00	0.01	0.43	0.90	0.75
Eastern Phoebe	0.00	<0.01	0.02	0.00	0.00	0.00	0.00	0.00	0.00
Eastern Wood-pewee	0.00	0.01	0.00	0.01	0.00	0.00	0.01	0.00	0.01
Field Sparrow	0.00	<0.01	0.00	0.00	0.00	0.00	0.00	0.00	0.01
Grasshopper Sparrow	**0.66**	**0.73**	**0.73**	**0.70**	**0.64**	**0.68**	**0.77**	**0.70**	**0.66**
Great blue Heron	0.01	<0.01	0.01	0.04	0.04	0.01	0.03	0.08	0.02
Great Crested Flycatcher	0.00	0.03	0.14	0.06	0.04	0.07	0.04	0.00	0.03
Great Horned Owl	0.00	<0.01	0.00	0.00	0.00	0.00	0.00	0.00	>0.01
Great-tailed Grackle	0.01	0.00	0.01	0.01	0.00	0.00	0.00	0.03	0.00
Greater Prairie-chicken	**0.01**	**0.02**	**0.01**	**0.00**	**0.01**	**0.00**	**0.01**	**0.00**	**0.05**
Hairy Woodpecker	0.01	0.00	0.00	0.00	0.00	0.00	0.00	0.00	0.00
Henslow's Sparrow	**0.00**	**0.00**	**0.00**	**0.00**	**0.01**	**0.01**	**0.09**	**0.10**	**0.08**
Horned Lark	0.02	0.00	0.28	0.11	0.12	0.06	0.00	0.03	0.04
Indigo Bunting	**0.00**	**<0.01**	**0.00**	**0.00**	**0.00**	**0.00**	**0.00**	**0.00**	**0.00**

Table 3. Proportion of plots occupied annually by breeding bird species (including flyovers) at Tallgrass Prairie National Preserve, Kansas during the 2001-2010 (excluding 2003) breeding bird surveys, by habitat type (continued).

Common name	Proportion of plots occupied								
	Grassland								
	2001	2002	2004	2005	2006	2007	2008	2009	2010
	n=158	n=242	n=81	n=79	n=81	n=71	n=77	n=40	n=242
Killdeer	0.06	0.11	0.17	0.25	0.23	0.11	0.09	0.05	0.06
Lark Sparrow	0.01	0.07	0.04	0.08	0.02	0.11	0.08	0.00	0.02
Loggerhead Shrike	0.00	<0.01	0.00	0.00	0.00	0.00	0.00	0.00	0.00
Mallard	0.00	0.00	0.00	0.00	0.00	0.00	0.00	0.00	>0.01
Mourning Dove	0.07	0.06	0.01	0.01	0.02	0.04	0.08	0.10	0.05
Northern Bobwhite	0.00	0.04	0.05	0.10	0.14	0.08	0.05	0.28	0.05
Northern Cardinal	0.00	0.05	0.01	0.03	0.01	0.03	0.00	0.00	>0.01
Northern Flicker	0.00	<0.01	0.01	0.00	0.00	0.00	0.00	0.03	0.00
Northern Harrier	0.00	0.00	0.00	0.01	0.00	0.01	0.00	0.00	0.01
Northern Mockingbird	0.00	0.00	0.00	0.03	0.01	0.01	0.00	0.05	>0.01
Northern Oriole	0.00	0.00	0.00	0.04	0.02	0.06	0.06	0.03	0.01
Northern Rough-winged Swallow	0.01	0.00	0.00	0.00	0.00	0.00	0.00	0.00	>0.01
Orchard Oriole	0.01	0.01	0.00	0.00	0.06	0.00	0.01	0.00	0.04
Pied-billed Grebe	0.00	0.00	0.00	0.00	0.01	0.00	0.00	0.00	0.00
Red-bellied Woodpecker	**0.01**	**0.04**	**0.02**	**0.03**	**0.00**	**0.01**	**0.13**	**0.00**	**0.00**
Red-headed Woodpecker	**0.00**	**0.00**	**0.00**	**0.03**	**0.04**	**0.00**	**0.00**	**0.03**	**>0.01**
Red-tailed Hawk	0.00	0.00	0.01	0.01	0.00	0.01	0.00	0.00	0.00
Red-winged Blackbird	0.06	0.22	0.26	0.20	0.25	0.20	0.00	0.25	0.16
Ring-necked Pheasant	0.00	0.00	0.00	0.00	0.00	0.00	0.00	0.03	0.00
Scissor-tailed Flycatcher	0.00	0.01	0.04	0.03	0.05	0.04	0.00	0.00	0.00
Tufted Titmouse	0.00	0.06	0.02	0.00	0.02	0.03	0.01	0.00	0.01
Turkey Vulture	0.01	0.01	0.01	0.01	0.04	0.01	0.03	0.13	0.05
Upland Sandpiper	0.27	0.72	0.75	0.57	0.60	0.46	0.40	0.48	0.26
Western Kingbird	0.02	0.00	0.00	0.00	0.00	0.00	0.00	0.00	>0.01
Western Meadowlark	0.23	0.90	0.88	0.85	0.89	0.83	0.42	0.00	0.03
White-breasted Nuthatch	0.00	0.02	0.00	0.01	0.00	0.00	0.00	0.00	0.00
White-eyed Vireo	**0.00**	**0.00**	**0.00**	**0.00**	**0.00**	**0.00**	**0.00**	**0.00**	**0.01**
Wild Turkey	0.00	<0.01	0.01	0.00	0.00	0.00	0.00	0.00	0.02
Yellow-billed Cuckoo	0.00	0.04	0.02	0.00	0.00	0.00	0.00	0.00	0.00
Yellow-breasted Chat	0.00	0.02	0.00	0.00	0.00	0.00	0.00	0.00	0.00
Yellow-throated Vireo	**0.00**	**<0.01**	**0.01**	**0.00**	**0.00**	**0.00**	**0.00**	**0.00**	**0.00**
Yellow Warbler	0.01	0.00	0.00	0.00	0.00	0.00	0.00	0.00	0.00

Table 3. Proportion of plots occupied annually by breeding bird species (including flyovers) at Tallgrass Prairie National Preserve, Kansas during the 2001-2010 (excluding 2003) breeding bird surveys, by habitat type (continued).

Common name	Proportion of plots occupied								
	Riparian								
	2001	2002	2004	2005	2006	2007	2008	2009	2010
	n=18	n=18	n=16	n=18	n=18	n=18	n=18	n=18	n=18
Acadian Flycatcher	**0.00**	**0.28**	**0.00**	**0.00**	**0.00**	**0.00**	**0.00**	**0.00**	**0.00**
American Crow	0.06	0.22	0.00	0.06	0.06	0.06	0.06	0.06	0.00
American Goldfinch	0.06	0.00	0.00	0.00	0.00	0.00	0.00	0.00	0.11
American Robin	0.00	0.00	0.06	0.00	0.00	0.00	0.00	0.17	0.11
Bank Swallow	0.00	0.00	0.06	0.00	0.00	0.00	0.06	0.00	0.06
Barn Swallow	0.00	0.00	0.00	0.06	0.00	0.00	0.00	0.00	0.00
Barred Owl	0.06	0.00	0.00	0.00	0.00	0.00	0.00	0.00	0.00
Belted Kingfisher	0.06	0.00	0.06	0.06	0.00	0.06	0.06	0.00	0.06
Bewick's Wren	0.11	0.11	0.06	0.06	0.00	0.11	0.06	0.00	0.00
Black-billed Cuckoo	0.06	0.06	0.00	0.33	0.00	0.00	0.00	0.00	0.00
Black-capped Chickadee	0.06	0.33	0.25	0.11	0.00	0.00	0.00	0.06	0.00
Blue-gray Gnatcatcher	0.06	0.00	0.13	0.28	0.22	0.17	0.28	0.06	0.11
Blue Grosbeak	0.00	0.00	0.13	0.00	0.00	0.00	0.06	0.00	0.00
Blue Jay	0.11	0.11	0.13	0.33	0.17	0.11	0.11	0.17	0.06
Brown-headed Cowbird	0.06	0.00	0.00	0.00	0.00	0.06	0.06	0.11	0.00
Brown Thrasher	**0.06**	**0.00**	**0.00**	**0.00**	**0.00**	**0.00**	**0.00**	**0.06**	**0.00**
Canada Goose	0.00	0.00	0.00	0.00	0.00	0.06	0.00	0.00	0.00
Carolina Chickadee	0.00	0.00	0.00	0.00	0.00	0.00	0.11	0.00	0.06
Carolina Wren	**0.17**	**0.00**	**0.00**	**0.11**	**0.11**	**0.11**	**0.06**	**0.00**	**0.06**
Cliff Swallow	0.00	0.06	0.00	0.00	0.00	0.00	0.00	0.00	0.00
Common Nighthawk	0.00	0.06	0.00	0.00	0.00	0.00	0.00	0.00	0.00
Common Yellowthroat	0.00	0.17	0.00	0.00	0.00	0.00	0.06	0.00	0.06
Dickcissel	**0.00**	**0.17**	**0.00**	**0.11**	**0.11**	**0.17**	**0.06**	**0.33**	**0.22**
Downy Woodpecker	0.11	0.22	0.00	0.00	0.00	0.00	0.06	0.00	0.06
Eastern Bluebird	0.00	0.00	0.00	0.06	0.11	0.06	0.00	0.11	0.00
Eastern Kingbird	0.00	0.00	0.00	0.00	0.00	0.00	0.06	0.00	0.00
Eastern Meadowlark	0.00	0.00	0.00	0.00	0.00	0.00	0.00	0.11	0.06
Eastern Phoebe	0.00	0.11	0.19	0.06	0.06	0.06	0.06	0.11	0.00
Eastern Wood-pewee	0.33	0.56	0.44	0.72	0.78	0.72	0.22	0.72	0.56
Gray Catbird	0.06	0.00	0.00	0.06	0.00	0.00	0.00	0.00	0.00
Great Blue Heron	0.00	0.00	0.00	0.00	0.00	0.06	0.00	0.17	0.06
Great Crested Flycatcher	0.22	0.22	0.75	0.56	0.61	0.44	0.17	0.22	0.28
Great Horned Owl	0.00	0.00	0.00	0.06	0.00	0.00	0.00	0.00	0.00
Hairy Woodpecker	0.00	0.00	0.19	0.06	0.06	0.00	0.00	0.06	0.00
House Wren	0.00	0.00	0.00	0.00	0.00	0.00	0.00	0.00	0.00
Indigo Bunting	**0.06**	**0.11**	**0.00**	**0.00**	**0.00**	**0.11**	**0.39**	**0.11**	**0.06**
Lark Sparrow	0.00	0.00	0.00	0.00	0.00	0.00	0.06	0.00	0.00
Mourning Dove	0.00	0.00	0.00	0.06	0.00	0.06	0.17	0.11	0.00

Table 3. Proportion of plots occupied annually by breeding bird species (including flyovers) at Tallgrass Prairie National Preserve, Kansas during the 2001-2010 (excluding 2003) breeding bird surveys, by habitat type (continued).

Common name	Proportion of plots occupied								
	Riparian								
	2001	2002	2004	2005	2006	2007	2008	2009	2010
	n=18	n=18	n=16	n=18	n=18	n=18	n=18	n=18	n=18
Northern Bobwhite	0.00	0.00	0.00	0.00	0.00	0.00	0.00	0.06	0.00
Northern Cardinal	0.17	0.28	0.13	0.28	0.17	0.28	0.17	0.39	0.17
Northern Flicker	0.00	0.00	0.00	0.06	0.00	0.00	0.00	0.39	0.00
Northern Mockingbird	0.00	0.00	0.00	0.00	0.00	0.00	0.06	0.00	0.00
Northern Oriole	0.00	0.00	0.00	0.17	0.28	0.00	0.06	0.22	0.00
Northern Rough-winged Swallow	0.00	0.00	0.00	0.00	0.00	0.00	0.00	0.00	0.06
Orchard Oriole	0.06	0.06	0.06	0.00	0.06	0.00	0.00	0.00	0.06
Prothonotary Warbler	**0.11**	**0.00**	**0.00**	**0.00**	**0.00**	**0.00**	**0.00**	**0.00**	**0.06**
Red-bellied Woodpecker	**0.17**	**0.39**	**0.19**	**0.22**	**0.33**	**0.17**	**0.28**	**0.11**	**0.17**
Red-eyed Vireo	0.00	0.22	0.19	0.17	0.28	0.22	0.11	0.06	0.17
Red-headed Woodpecker	**0.00**	**0.06**	**0.13**	**0.00**	**0.00**	**0.00**	**0.00**	**0.11**	**0.00**
Red-tailed Hawk	0.00	0.00	0.06	0.00	0.06	0.00	0.00	0.00	0.00
Red-winged Blackbird	0.00	0.06	0.06	0.00	0.00	0.06	0.00	0.00	0.00
Ruby-throated Hummingbird	0.00	0.00	0.00	0.06	0.00	0.00	0.00	0.00	0.00
Tufted Titmouse	0.06	0.44	0.44	0.17	0.39	0.39	0.11	0.00	0.33
Turkey Vulture	0.00	0.00	0.06	0.00	0.00	0.00	0.00	0.06	0.11
Western Meadowlark	0.00	0.11	0.19	0.00	0.06	0.00	0.00	0.00	0.00
White-breasted Nuthatch	0.00	0.39	0.06	0.17	0.28	0.17	0.11	0.11	0.11
White-eyed Vireo	**0.17**	**0.00**	**0.00**	**0.00**	**0.00**	**0.00**	**0.00**	**0.00**	**0.00**
Wild Turkey	0.00	0.00	0.06	0.06	0.00	0.11	0.00	0.06	0.00
Yellow-billed Cuckoo	0.11	0.28	0.50	0.00	0.00	0.00	0.22	0.17	0.00
Yellow-breasted Chat	0.00	0.00	0.00	0.00	0.00	0.06	0.00	0.00	0.00
Yellow-throated Vireo	**0.06**	**0.06**	**0.13**	**0.17**	**0.00**	**0.06**	**0.17**	**0.11**	**0.11**
Yellow Warbler	0.17	0.00	0.25	0.11	0.22	0.00	0.06	0.00	0.06

Bolded species names are those species considered of continental importance (Rich et al. 2004).

Bird Habitat

Habitats on grassland plots consist primarily of the upland prairie type, with much lesser amounts of other types present (Table 4). Habitats on riparian plots consist primarily of the riparian woodland and stream types, with lesser amounts of other types present (Table 5). Canopy cover averaged ~83% on riparian plots, with cover provided by hardwood trees. Canopy cover was minimal (< 1%) on grassland plots. Basal area from hardwood trees in the riparian area averaged 8.06 m^2 / ha on plots. Hardwood tree species from 16 different families contributed to the canopy cover and basal area (Table 5).

On grassland plots, maximum vegetation height average 0.39 m across year (Table 4). However, it should be noted that maximum vegetation height and variability increased in later years of monitoring with vegetation cover recorded in all horizontal profile height classes below 1.75 m when read from 15 m. Vegetation was recorded in all horizontal profile height classes to 2.0 m on riparian plots (Table 5). Average vertical structure diversity estimates across years averaged ~10% across grassland plots, and ~26% across riparian plots.

Grass litter was the dominate litter type recorded on grassland plots across years, with deciduous litter the dominant litter type on riparian plots (Table 4 and 5). Plots were primarily unvegetated at ground level in both grassland and riparian areas. On grassland plots, warm season-grasses and forbs dominated the forage guilds during our late-May early-June bird surveys across years. On riparian plots, cool-season grasses, forbs, and woody shrubs and vines dominated the forage guilds across years. Total foliar coverage averaged ~46% across plots sampled in grassland areas, and ~39% in riparian areas.

Table 4. Averages (± std dev) for habitat parameters in the grasslands at Tallgrass Prairie National Preserve, Kansas during the bird breeding seasons, 2001–2010 (excluding 2003, 2009). Within the scale in which habitat parameters are collected, 50-m plot, 5-m subplot, and 1.78-m sample plot, percentages of coverage may not necessarily sum to 100% as values are averaged over mid-point values of cover classes (i.e. class 1 = 0.5%, class 2 = 3.0%, class 3 = 15.0%, class 4 = 37.5%, class 5 = 62.5%, class 6 = 85.0%, and class 7 = 97.5%).

Habitat Parameter	2001	2002	2004	2005	2006	2007	2008	2010
50 meter plot coverage								
Brome field (%)	1.85 (13.35)	3.24 (17.47)	6.02 (23.61)	7.41 (25.99)	3.61 (18.53)	4.12 (19.75)	3.80 (18.99)	2.79 (16.09)
Drainage (%)	--	>0.01 (0.03)	0.65 (4.47)	0.19 (1.69)	--	0.65 (4.48)	1.58 (5.58)	0.40 (2.81)
Intermittent water cover (%)	0.27 (2.99)							
Upland prairie (%)	93.88 (17.36)	92.61 (19.69)	85.12 (27.44)	86.90 (27.41)	92.81 (18.65)	87.96 (21.93)	88.57 (22.05)	91.14 (17.40)
Pasture road (%)	0.55 (2.43)	0.32 (1.53)	0.70 (2.90)	0.32 (1.77)	0.31 (1.75)	0.30 (1.84)	0.66 (2.49)	0.25 (0.83)
Pond (%)	0.59 (4.37)	0.43 (3.65)	1.39 (7.13)	0.23 (1.72)	0.39 (2.34)	0.22 (1.78)	0.49 (4.27)	0.39 (3.53)
Riparian prairie (%)				1.34 (8.16)			0.76 (4.60)	
Riparian woodland (%)	0.12 (1.22)	0.18 (1.41)	0.25 (1.70)	0.01 (0.06)	0.12 (0.57)	0.01 (0.06)	0.19 (1.71)	0.17 (2.42)
Seep (%)				0.04 (0.34)				
Shrub (%)	0.03 (0.25)	0.08 (0.98)		0.95 (5.93)			0.05 (0.35)	
Stream (%)	0.41 (2.10)	0.80 (4.65)	0.67 (2.88)	1.04 (3.35)	0.41 (1.80)	0.60 (2.57)	0.72 (2.95)	0.24 (0.81)
5 meter subplot								
Canopy cover								
Hardwood (%)	0.00	0.44 (6.12)	0.00	0.05 (0.47)	0.77 (6.96)	0.00	0.36 (3.20)	0.01 (0.12)
Total cover (%)	0.00	0.44 (6.12)	0.00	0.05 (0.47)	0.77 (6.96)	0.00	0.36 (3.20)	0.01 (0.12)
Canopy Height								
Hardwood (m)	0.10 (1.24)	0.13 (1.16)	0.10 (0.89)	0.10 (0.90)	0.16 (1.44)	0.00	0.16 (1.41)	0.09 (0.97)
Basal area								
Hardwood (m²/ha)	0.02 (0.24)	0.04 (0.32)	0.00	0.03 (0.16)	0.07 (0.57)	0.00	0.03 (0.23)	0.02 (0.13)
Total (m²/ha)	0.02 (0.24)	0.04 (0.32)	0.00	0.03 (0.16)	0.07 (0.57)	0.00	0.03 (0.23)	0.02 (0.13)
Horizontal vegetation profile at 15-m								
0.00 – 0.25 m (%)					67.60 (30.61)	71.90 (24.30)	91.27 (12.23)	78.51 (23.26)
0.00 – 0.50 m (%)	82.29 (24.41)	65.47 (30.12)	61.99 (31.72)	53.73 (28.90)				
0.25 – 0.50 m (%)					12.34 (23.43)	16.97 (30.52)	46.27 (39.51)	37.57 (37.99)
0.25 – 0.75 m (%)			18.02 (29.01)	10.46 (25.63)				
0.50 – 0.75 m (%)					2.51 (12.40)	5.63 (20.50)	5.66 (21.72)	3.97 (14.21)
0.50 – 1.00 m (%)	4.10 (14.30)	4.52 (18.50)	2.97 (13.50)	1.38 (6.33)				
0.75 – 1.00 m (%)					0.66 (4.47)	0.43 (2.50)	4.68 (20.10)	0.66 (3.79)
0.75 – 1.25 m (%)			0.66 (4.47)	0.00				
1.00 – 1.25 m (%)					0.00	0.00	3.64 (18.22)	0.05 (0.29)
1.00 – 1.50 m (%)	0.01 (0.06)	0.09 (1.00)	0.00	0.19 (1.69)				
1.25 – 1.50 m (%)					0.00	0.00	0.04 (0.34)	>0.01 (0.05)
1.25 – 1.75 m (%)			0.00	0.19 (1.69)				
1.50 – 1.75 m (%)					0.00	0.00	0.00	0.00
1.50 – 2.00 m (%)	0.62 (7.82)	0.16 (2.44)	0.00	0.00				
1.75 – 2.00 m (%)					0.00	0.00	0.00	0.00
Maximum vegetation height (m)	0.45 (0.20)	0.36 (0.22)	0.35 (0.20)	0.29 (0.18)	0.36 (0.18)	0.40 (0.18)	0.47 (0.24)	0.41 (0.25)
Vertical structure diversity (%)	9.37 (1.16)	9.57 (1.60)	9.36 (0.56)	9.49 (0.65)	9.57 (1.56)	9.40 (0.44)	10.77 (5.46)	9.60 (0.66)

Table 4. Averages (± std dev) for habitat parameters in the grasslands at Tallgrass Prairie National Preserve, Kansas during the bird breeding seasons, 2001–2010 (excluding 2003, 2009). Within the scale in which habitat parameters are collected, 50-m plot, 5-m subplot, and 1.78-m sample plot, percentages of coverage may not necessarily sum to 100% as values are averaged over mid-point values of cover classes (i.e. class 1 = 0.5%, class 2 = 3.0%, class 3 = 15.0%, class 4 = 37.5%, class 5 = 62.5%, class 6 = 85.0%, and class 7 = 97.5%) (continued).

Habitat Parameter	2001	2002	2004	2005	2006	2007	2008	2010
				1.78 meter sample plot coverage				
Deciduous litter (%)	0.12 (1.22)	0.43 (0.98)	0.17 (0.58)	0.30 (0.25)	0.36 (0.38)	0.30 (0.52)	0.40 (0.37)	0.45 (0.60)
Grass litter (%)	9.59 (17.43)	28.53 (20.89)	11.45 (14.60)	7.30 (14.56)	9.57 (15.28)	29.58 (19.23)	23.36 (28.17)	26.92 (18.55)
Bare soil (%)	49.74 (21.22)	50.29 (23.47)	67.54 (16.92)	74.15 (16.70)	70.38 (22.22)	59.75 (15.66)	61.51 (26.94)	27.54 (14.27)
Rock (%)	7.11 (13.24)	7.50 (11.99)	10.79 (16.40)	8.34 (13.24)	7.91 (13.56)	9.05 (16.77)	3.11 (7.88)	8.87 (13.89)
Woody debris (%)	0.02 (0.24)	0.01 (0.06)	1.14 (9.44)	0.01 (0.06)	0.06 (0.34)	1.25 (10.09)	0.05 (0.35)	0.60 (1.70)
Unvegetated (%)	81.61 (9.06)	83.84 (9.95)	84.69 (15.26)	84.78 (8.83)	86.79 (12.24)	85.21 (3.73)	86.23 (6.72)	58.57 (11.13)
Warm-season grass (%)	20.03 (15.48)	38.94 (18.31)	25.21 (14.50)	25.40 (14.21)	17.67 (16.00)	31.89 (17.10)	20.04 (14.20)	32.08 (13.21)
Cool-season grass (%)	3.82 (11.46)	6.65 (16.87)	9.96 (14.77)	7.16 (16.55)	3.48 (10.87)	4.17 (15.92)	5.12 (12.30)	5.68 (10.01)
Forb (%)	20.68 (12.33)	9.56 (9.85)	17.35 (10.13)	15.34 (9.58)	8.20 (9.18)	10.50 (12.07)	8.60 (10.28)	15.23 (6.17)
Moss and lichen (%)	<0.01 (0.04)	0.48 (1.54)	1.53 (2.94)	0.99 (2.03)	0.33 (0.72)	0.31 (1.81)	0.26 (0.26)	0.61 (2.06)
Woody shrub and vine (%)	1.37 (7.85)	4.67 (7.07)	1.28 (5.01)	3.07 (4.26)	2.71 (4.03)	1.68 (3.11)	2.45 (3.25)	1.77 (3.91)
Tree seedling (%)	<0.01 (0.04)	0.01 (0.19)	0.00	0.00	0.04 (0.33)	0.04 (0.36)	0.00	0.00
Total foliar (%)	53.48 (19.45)	44.64 (17.34)	52.04 (16.21)	41.23 (14.75)	33.31 (20.18)	58.06 (14.65)	41.11 (13.25)	42.69 (12.50)

Table 5. Averages (± std dev) for habitat parameters in the riparian areas at Tallgrass Prairie National Preserve, Kansas during the bird breeding seasons, 2001–2010 (excluding 2003, 2009). Within the scale in which habitat parameters are collected, 50-m plot, 5-m subplot, and 1.78-m sample plot, percentages of coverage may not necessarily sum to 100% as values are averaged over mid-point values of cover classes (i.e. class 1 = 0.5%, class 2 = 3.0%, class 3 = 15.0%, class 4 = 37.5%, class 5 = 62.5%, class 6 = 85.0%, and class 7 = 97.5%).

Habitat Parameter	2001	2002	2004	2005	2006	2007	2008	2010
50 meter plot coverage								
Brome field (%)	--	3.14 (9.28)	9.91 (18.96)	11.44 (24.76)	5.83 (12.49)	0.17 (0.71)	4.53 (12.03)	2.92 (9.32)
Corn field (%)	--	--	--	--	2.08 (8.84)	1.00 (3.56)	--	--
Field/prairie	--	--	--	--	--	--	0.03 (0.12)	--
Upland prairie (%)	--	2.08 (8.84)	5.41 (15.69)	8.81 (21.29)	1.83 (4.84)	0.17 (0.71)	8.83 (21.28)	2.92 (9.32)
Old field (%)	--	--	--	--	--	--	0.83 (3.54)	--
Pasture road (%)	--	--	--	--	0.17 (0.71)	0.03 (0.11)	0.03 (0.12)	0.17 (0.71)
Restored prairie (%)	--	--	--	2.08 (8.84)	2.08 (8.84)	2.08 (8.84)	2.08 (8.84)	--
Riparian prairie (%)	--	--	--	--	--	--	8.36 (24.11)	--
Riparian woodland (%)	97.50 (0.00)	88.19 (17.08)	72.03 (26.60)	67.81 (30.78)	58.75 (27.74)	60.56 (25.92)	42.64 (27.81)	79.44 (11.20)
Shrub (%)	--	--	2.53 (9.36)	0.03 (0.12)	--	--	0.17 (0.71)	--
Stream (%)	20.14 (15.19)	24.17 (12.75)	18.46 (9.90)	30.00 (10.91)	27.92 (12.81)	23.58 (22.35)	31.25 (10.37)	10.06 (19.42)
5 meter subplot								
Canopy cover								
Hardwood (%)	80.66 (21.47)	66.37 (18.45)	85.04 (14.00)	88.00 (18.22)	85.67 (16.17)	85.10 (16.92)	87.65 (21.19)	89.32 (18.33)
Total cover (%)	80.66 (21.47)	66.37 (18.45)	85.04 (14.00)	88.00 (18.22)	85.67 (16.17)	85.10 (16.92)	87.65 (21.19)	89.32 (18.33)
Canopy height								
Hardwood (m)	17.69 (10.11)	20.85 (7.07)	24.27 (9.40)	16.81 (7.07)	20.96 (7.62)	16.61 (7.44)	21.61 (7.83)	21.10 (11.00)
Basal Area								
Hardwood (m^2/ha)	7.83 (4.22)	7.28 (3.37)	6.38 (4.13)	8.50 (4.50)	8.78 (4.37)	7.94 (4.26)	8.17 (3.91)	9.56 (4.54)
Total (m^2/ha)	7.83 (4.22)	7.28 (3.37)	6.38 (4.13)	8.50 (4.50)	8.78 (4.37)	7.94 (4.26)	8.17 (3.91)	9.56 (4.54)
Horizontal vegetation profile at 15-m								
0.00 – 0.25 m (%)	--	--	93.75 (9.35)	80.42 (33.22)	97.7 (0.00)	94.17 (14.14)	97.50 (0.00)	97.5 (0.00)
0.00 – 0.50 m (%)	90.28 (17.34)	92.25 (22.27)	--	--	--	--	--	--
0.25 – 0.50 m (%)	--	--	75.81 (35.97)	70.22 (40.25)	90.14 (15.94)	78.22 (32.64)	96.81 (2.95)	92.08 (14.43)
0.25 – 0.75 m (%)	--	--	--	--	--	--	--	--
0.50 – 0.75 m (%)	--	--	36.30 (36.40)	32.00 (36.60)	53.30 (44.10)	51.80 (43.80)	48.31 (41.88)	58.53 (38.67)
0.50 – 1.00 m (%)	48.20 (35.30)	43.30 (39.30)	--	--	--	--	--	--
0.75 – 1.00 m (%)	--	--	17.22 (29.32)	17.25 (33.60)	24.50 (33.88)	30.28 (39.42)	25.30 (37.60)	26.97 (38.34)
0.75 – 1.25 m (%)	--	--	--	--	--	--	--	--
1.00 – 1.25 m (%)	--	--	8.63 (25.50)	21.40 (35.40)	12.20 (27.00)	21.40 (32.40)	17.56 (33.45)	21.17 (40.36)
1.00 – 1.50 m (%)	9.81 (26.50)	10.10 (26.40)	--	--	--	--	--	--
1.25 – 1.50 m (%)	--	--	8.63 (25.47)	18.36 (31.30)	15.19 (33.42)	23.14 (36.29)	10.40 (25.00)	16.28 (37.38)
1.25 – 1.75 m (%)	--	--	--	--	--	--	--	--
1.50 – 1.75 m (%)	--	--	2.38 (9.50)	19.50 (33.70)	19.80 (34.60)	28.20 (42.30)	11.31 (23.21)	21.97 (38.46)
1.50 – 2.00 m (%)	14.90 (25.00)	15.20 (29.30)	--	--	--	--	--	--
1.75 – 2.00 m (%)	--	--	--	--	--	--	16.80 (28.60)	26.00 (39.57)
Vertical structure diversity (%)	27.65 (9.42)	24.35 (5.64)	24.22 (6.52)	21.49 (4.59)	22.19 (7.33)	27.91 (12.56)	27.60 (12.32)	30.90 (11.83)

20

Table 5. Averages (± std dev) for habitat parameters in the riparian areas at Tallgrass Prairie National Preserve, Kansas during the bird breeding seasons, 2001-2010 (excluding 2003, 2009). Within the scale in which habitat parameters are collected, 50-m plot, 5-m subplot, and 1.78-m sample plot, percentages of coverage may not necessarily sum to 100% as values are averaged over mid-point values of cover classes (i.e. class 1 = 0.5%, class 2 = 3.0%, class 3 = 15.0%, class 4 = 37.5%, class 5 = 62.5%, class 6 = 85.0%, and class 7 = 97.5%) (continued).

Habitat Parameter	2001	2002	2004	2005	2006	2007	2008	2010
			1.78 meter sample plot coverage					
Deciduous litter (%)	36.36 (28.68)	43.00 (24.81)	14.72 (15.69)	17.25 (18.67)	42.00 (26.77)	20.69 (20.97)	62.22 (26.67)	34.08 (18.09)
Grass litter (%)	4.67 (9.40)	7.72 (14.89)	6.91 (10.24)	7.75 (14.53)	3.58 (9.14)	10.92 (19.54)	4.64 (14.49)	14.86 (13.85)
Bare soil (%)	35.11 (27.76)	22.92 (29.50)	67.50 (20.25)	66.42 (25.09)	52.94 (26.74)	54.75 (18.42)	17.78 (22.01)	14.25 (7.39)
Rock (%)	1.22 (3.57)	3.50 (6.36)	2.31 (5.00)	4.92 (9.87)	3.58 (9.17)	2.50 (8.79)	1.94 (4.80)	2.72 (4.62)
Woody debris (%)	4.11 (9.02)	5.89 (6.70)	9.59 (6.36)	5.19 (5.50)	4.11 (5.16)	5.94 (14.87)	2.67 (3.33)	7.58 (9.04)
Unvegetated (%)	82.67 (24.22)	82.64 (14.94)	79.69 (14.63)	70.00 (15.51)	83.61 (14.53)	88.47 (5.76)	89.86 (6.27)	59.58 (11.45)
Warm-season grass (%)	0.94 (3.51)	1.69 (4.84)	2.16 (5.07)	3.86 (9.67)	1.89 (4.82)	5.31 (9.71)	0.22 (0.71)	3.19 (5.57)
Cool-season grass (%)	13.17 (14.67)	21.89 (26.08)	13.72 (17.65)	26.81 (21.90)	17.31 (14.25)	17.86 (22.69)	14.03 (15.75)	19.42 (15.75)
Forb (%)	10.50 (9.37)	15.44 (13.61)	20.63 (10.06)	14.89 (14.61)	14.97 (17.61)	6.36 (6.39)	6.72 (6.07)	15.58 (6.16)
Moss and lichen (%)	0.00	0.61 (0.90)	3.44 (5.85)	1.19 (3.58)	1.22 (3.57)	0.03 (0.12)	0.47 (0.67)	0.06 (0.16)
Woody shrub and vine (%)	9.31 (24.02)	6.83 (12.48)	10.63 (14.43)	9.33 (11.94)	7.28 (11.84)	2.67 (5.72)	6.44 (9.72)	6.03 (9.39)
Tree seedling (%)	0.22 (0.26)	0.97 (1.31)	1.13 (3.77)	0.00	0.64 (1.11)	1.78 (3.55)	2.69 (5.67)	2.50 (4.74)
Total foliar (%)	36.86 (25.77)	33.36 (21.15)	42.81 (23.22)	43.61 (19.33)	43.47 (17.58)	38.06 (16.30)	34.89 (22.01)	39.75 (13.23)

Table 6. Stems per hectare of trees found in the riparian area on Tallgrass Prairie National Preserve, Kansas by size class, during the 2001-2010(excluding 2003, 2009) bird-breeding seasons. Stems per hectare of trees are reported by family.

Family	<1.0 cm	1.1 – 2.5 cm	2.6 – 8.0 cm	8.1 – 15.0 cm	15.1 – 23.0 cm	23.1 – 38.0 cm	>38.0 cm
Aceraceae	0	0	0	7	0	7	0
Anacardiaceae	0	7	0	0	0	0	0
Cornaceae	87	40	27	0	7	0	0
Fabaceae	0	7	21	14	7	7	8
Fagaceae	7	7	11	11	7	7	7
Hippocastanaceae	0	0	22	11	7	0	0
Juglandaceae	0	14	14	15	14	7	8
Magnoliaceae	0	0	0	0	7	0	0
Oleacea	0	7	11	17	16	11	8
Platanaceae	0	0	0	7	7	7	14
Rosaceae	0	7	0	0	0	0	0
Rutaceae	7	0	0	0	0	0	0
Salicaceae	78	50	35	24	25	28	35
Sapindaceae	0	0	14	0	0	0	0
Tiliaceae	0	0	0	0	0	7	0
Ulmaceae	28	13	78	80	61	75	32
Total stems	**207**	**152**	**233**	**186**	**158**	**156**	**112**
Snags	0	14	11	16	13	7	0

Summary

Bird surveys and habitat assessment work were initiated at Tallgrass Prairie National Preserve, Kansas, in 2001, to assist the park in assessing the ecological integrity of habitat on the Preserve through time. Eighty-two of the 97 bird species recorded are permanent or summer residents to the area (Stokes and Stokes 1996). Current efforts to restore and maintain the grassland and riparian habitats at TAPR should provide a diversity of habitats necessary to meet the varied requirements of the 13 breeding species of continental importance observed. Efforts to restore and maintain the grassland habitats will also provide the diversity of habitats necessary to meet the varied requirements of the nine breeding species classified as grassland obligates.

Literature Cited

Cairns Jr., J., P. V. McCormick, and B. R. Niederlehner. 2004. A proposed framework for developing indicators of ecosystem health. Hydrobiologia 263:1-44.

Fancy, S.G. 1997. A new approach for analyzing bird densities from variable circular-plot counts. Pacific Science 51:107-114.

ITIS (Integrated Taxonomic Information System). Accessed in 2010, http://www.itis.usda.gov/.

Karr, J. R. 1991. Biological integrity: a long-neglected aspect of water resource management. Ecological Applications 1:66-84.

Karr, J. R., and D. R. Dudley. 1981. Ecological perspective on water quality goals. Environmental Management 5:55-68.

Mallory, M. L., H. G. Gilchrist, B. M. Braune, and A. J. Gaston. 2006. Marine birds as indicators of arctic marine ecosystem health: linking the northern ecosystem initiative to long-term studies. Environmental Monitoring and Assessment 113:31-48.

Maurer, B. A. 1993. Biological diversity, ecological integrity, and neotropical migrants: New perspectives for wildlife managers. Pages 24-31 *in* D.M. Finch and P.W. Stangel, editors. Status and management of neotropical migratory birds. U.S. Forest Service General Technical Report RM-229.

Northern Prairie Wildlife Research Center. 2009. Northern Prairie Wildlife Research Center-online. Online. (http://www.npwrc.usgs.gov/). Accessed 10 September 2009.

Peitz, D.G., G.A. Rowell, J.L. Haack, K.M. James, L.W. Morrison, and M.D. Debacker. 2008. Breeding bird monitoring protocol for the Heartland Network Inventory and Monitoring Program. Natural Resource Report NPS/HTLN/NRR-2008/044. National Park Service, Fort Collins, Colorado. 152pp.

Peitz, D. G., M. M. Guck, and J. M. James. 2010. Bird monitoring at Tallgrass Prairie National Preserve, Kansas: 2001-2008 status report. Natural Resource Technical Report NPS/HTLN/NRTR—2010/318. National Park Service, Fort Collins, Colorado.

Rich, T.D., C.J. Beardmore, H. Berlanga, P.J. Blancher, M.S.W. Bradstreet, G.S. Butcher, D.W. Demarest, E.H. Dunn, W.C. Hunter, E.E. Inigo-Elias, J.A. Kennedy, A.M. Martell. A.O. Panjabi, D.N. Pashley, K.V. Rosenberg, C.M. Rustay, J.S. Wendt, T.C. Will. 2004. Partners in Flight North American Landbird Conservation Plan. Cornell Lab of Ornithology, Ithaca, New York. 84pp.

Stokes, D.W. and L.Q. Stokes. 1996. Stokes Field Guide to Birds: Eastern Region. Little, Brown and Company, New York, New York. 471 pp.

Wood, J. K., N. Nur, C. A. Howell, and G. R. Geupel. 2006. Overview of Cosumnes riparian bird study and recommendations for monitoring and management. A Report to the California Bay-Delta Authority Ecosystem Restoration Program. Petaluma, California. 18pp.